Original title:
The Meaning of Life (and Other Mysteries)

Copyright © 2025 Creative Arts Management OÜ
All rights reserved.

Author: Nash Everly
ISBN HARDBACK: 978-1-80566-233-4
ISBN PAPERBACK: 978-1-80566-528-1

Tapestry of Time

We weave our dreams with mismatched threads,
Stitching up tales where laughter spreads.
A sock, a shoe, a pie from the sky,
Life's a circus! Who needs to fly?

In purple pants and polka-dot hats,
We dance with squirrels and chat with cats.
The clock goes tick, but we lose the race,
Chasing the fun in life's silly space.

Secrets in the Stars

Stars wink at us with a cheeky grin,
Whispers of secrets, where do we begin?
A cosmic joke, or just a prank?
Is Pluto still in, or is it just dank?

In puddles of stardust, we splash and slide,
Mapping out dreams on a galactic ride.
Asteroids laugh, while comets glide,
Who knew the universe had a fun side?

Labyrinth of Wonders

Enter the maze where the cheese does dance,
Every turn's a riddle, or a chance!
Tickling the walls, with candy canes,
Finding joy even when it rains.

With every twist, we meet a goat,
Who sings a tune from an old wooden boat.
Chasing down echoes, let's giggle and spin,
In a world where the fun never wears thin.

Ephemeral Paths of Purpose

Life's a bubble, bright and round,
Floating on whims, never quite bound.
Purpose is like a ticklish sneeze,
It comes and it goes, just like a breeze.

With rubber ducks and a jazz band tune,
We aim for the stars, but stick to the moon.
Navigating chaos with a silly grin,
In this short ride, let the fun begin!

Underground Rivers of Truth

Down in the dark, where giggles flow,
Rivers of whispers, secrets in tow.
Fish wearing hats swim past the sighs,
Bubbling laughter, no one knows why.

Ducks in tuxedos debate all night,
Over the wonders of socks and flight.
A frog with a crown takes the lead,
While the jokes take root like a humble seed.

Spaces Between the Stars

In the gaps where stardust plays,
Aliens argue in cosmic cafes.
Eating rainbow cake with a twist,
Hoping a black hole won't ruin their list.

Planets dance in a waltz so grand,
While comets throw parties, isn't it planned?
Quasars chuckle, flaring their light,
As the universe spins, causing delight.

Constellations of Possibility

Orion lost his pants, what a sight!
Jupiter scribbles on cosmic heights.
And Mars swears he'll join in the fun,
While Venus serenades, not one to shun.

Stars debate the best ice cream flavor,
Pluto pouts, claiming he's the savior.
But even black holes can't help but frown,
When humor's the crown of a universal town.

Beneath the Surface of Now

Under the waves, where silliness lurks,
Mermaids craft tales with giggles and quirks.
Seahorses tango, tails tightly spun,
As octopuses juggle for fun.

Crabs in a conga line crinkle and clap,
While clowns on coral bring joy to the map.
The ocean's a playground, with bubbles to blow,
Finding delight in the ebb and the flow.

Questions Hanging in the Breeze

Why does cheese smell like feet?
Is there truth behind that kitchen beat?
Cats stare like they know the score,
While dogs just chase that open door.

Are socks the lost friends of shoes?
And why can't we pick our own news?
Why does water stay in the cup?
Is it waiting for someone to sup?

Do clouds play tag in the sky?
And why don't we just learn to fly?
Do fish think they swim in a pond,
Or do they dream of oceans beyond?

So many questions float in the air,
With laughter and joy so light and rare.
Let's ponder this with a light-hearted grin,
For life's a joke, let's all dive in!

As the World Turns

Why does the sun wake up so late?
Is it busy planning its grand estate?
The moon's got secrets, it whispers at night,
While stars just twinkle, oh what a sight!

Do trees gossip when no one is near?
And what does a squirrel think of reindeer?
Is coffee just beans in a heated debate?
Or is it magic in a caffeinated state?

When does a sandwich become a delight?
Is it the crunch that makes it feel right?
Why do we shout at the TV screen?
As if the players know what we mean!

As the world spins round in a silly dance,
Let's ponder these thoughts, give laughter a chance.
Why is life's riddle wrapped in a jest?
Embrace the chaos and call it a quest!

Portrait of a Fleeting Moment

A raindrop hangs on the edge of a leaf,
An ant wonders if it's too short or brief.
Time ticks the rhythm of a fast-beating heart,
But what if it's just a sweet work of art?

A fleeting laugh in a crowded room,
Blows softly by like a sweet perfume.
A wink shared amid the day's busy strife,
Makes one wonder about the essence of life.

A cat leaps high for a sunbeam's embrace,
While a dog just chases its tail in a race.
Moments collide like stars in the night,
Making the ordinary feel just right.

Through every smile and every surprise,
Life dances along like butterflies.
Capture the now with a dash of flair,
For fleeting moments are treasures we share!

A Symphony of Unsung Stories

What if chairs could tell us their tales?
Of all the people who sat, shared our fails?
Do forks dream of spaghetti on plates,
While spoons wonder about soup's fateful states?

The clock ticks softly, what does it see?
Does it giggle at all our haste to be free?
A shoelace trips as it whispers goodbye,
To sneakers that dash as if they can fly.

The humble potato, so round and so meek,
Could tell of the fries that everyone seeks.
Do pencils talk of the words that they write?
Or is it a mystery lost in the night?

In this laughter-filled orchestra, let's hear,
The stories surrounding us, ever so near.
For life plays a tune with a whimsical beat,
As we dance through the day, embracing each feat!

Footprints on the Sands of Forever

In the sand, I left my shoes,
They wandered off for some fresh views.
The tide came in, oh what a laugh,
Now I'm barefoot on this sandy path.

I called to seagulls, said, "Hey, guys!"
They told me tales of fishy spies.
While searching for my missing pair,
I found a crab with quite the flair.

A beach ball bounced right by my feet,
It rolled away, oh such deceit!
I chased it down, but then it fled,
And left me wondering instead.

So here I stand, my toes in sun,
Just me and waves, we're having fun.
Though footprints fade, these laughs remain,
I'll find my shoes… well, maybe not again!

Serendipity in the Ordinary

I spilled my coffee, what a sight,
A splash of brown, morning delight.
The cat took a leap, slipped on the floor,
Now she's auditioning for cat folklore.

The toast popped up with a funny face,
Imitating my breakfast race.
I flipped it over, made it dance,
Turns out it had a taste for romance.

The mailbox squeaked, I felt it tease,
As I rifled through junk mail with ease.
Found a coupon for a giant pie,
Who knew my day would crumble and fly?

As I munched on crumbs, felt quite the twist,
Life's little quirks I couldn't resist.
Each moment's a riddle, cook it right,
Find joy in the ordinary's light.

The Palette of Human Experience

A splash of blue on Monday morn,
Chasing dreams that feel quite torn.
A stroke of red when tempers flare,
Life's an artist with shades to spare.

Green is for the lunch I hate,
From leafy greens, I contemplate.
Yellow smiles in sunny beams,
With giggles added to our dreams.

Purple moments of pure delight,
When friends gather for board game night.
Orange laughs over cheesy puns,
Life's a canvas with twists and runs.

So splash the colors, let them blend,
In this artwork, there's no end.
With every brush, the chaos sings,
In this grand mix, what joy it brings!

Guardians of the Soul's Journey

We're all just clowns on a big ol' stage,
Performing scripts in life's absurd cage.
Juggling dreams, tripping on fate,
Noses bright red, when will we relate?

The universe beams with a wink so sly,
While satellites watch as we skydive by.
Stars chuckle softly, planets take bets,
On each little diner and all the regrets.

We dance through life in mismatched shoes,
Sipping on wisdom, sipping on blues.
Our hearts are balloons, floating about,
And we're the guardians with laughter throughout.

So let's laugh loud, embrace the bizarre,
Join the parade, you're a shining star.
For life's tender chaos is sweetly spun,
In the end, we're just here to have fun!

The Ripple Effect of Being

If you drop a pebble, life will laugh,
Waves of giggles, a quirky path.
Frogs in tuxedos leap in delight,
Dancing in puddles under moonlight.

Chasing your tail, a curious quest,
Finding lost socks, as humor's best.
Socks have their secrets, they wisely hide,
In a world where logic might subside.

Bananas in trees, why not take a chance?
Plants with hoedowns lead the amusing dance.
Ever seen a cat chase its own tail?
An endless loop where sanity might pale.

So loosen your grip on what you know,
Let whimsy guide you where laughter will flow.
For in this odd journey, truth often bends,
And sometimes your laugh is where reason ends.

Heartbeats in the Void

In the silence, a heartbeat plays,
Pulsing like a disco in cosmic ways.
Stars waltz with planets, a nightly show,
While squirrels debate the best nut to stow.

A cosmic joke floats through the air,
Telling us life's just one big dare.
Can you measure joy with a grand old scale?
Or is it found in a funny old tale?

Frogs sing duets with crickets at night,
A chorus of laughter under the starlight.
What's the score? Who even keeps track?
In this bizarre symphony, a cosmic quack.

So next time you ponder the vast unknown,
Remember the joy in a funny bone.
Dance through the void with a skip and a hop,
Life's punchline will land, and we won't want to stop.

Sonnet of the Forgotten

Forgotten socks embrace dusty seams,
Worn-out shoes hum abandoned dreams.
Laughter echoes in the pantry of woe,
Where pickles and jelly conspire to grow.

Old chairs creak, sharing sage advice,
"Don't take life too seriously, roll the dice!"
A barrel of laughs in the attic stands,
While ghosts of the past host whimsical bands.

A mismatched puzzle, pieces all askew,
Life's not a straight line, more like a skew.
Drawing the curtain on yesterday's play,
Laughter's the ticket; come join the fray!

From dust and regrets, let giggles arise,
In the heart of the chaos, find your surprise.
For each little stumble, each blunder we face,
Can spin to a tale filled with humor and grace.

Portraits of Perception

Upon a canvas where dreams run wild,
Life paints confusion, like a lost child.
Splatters of joy, in colors so strange,
Reality's brush makes the oddest change.

A rabbit in bow ties, sipping his tea,
Asks, "Why does time never wait for me?"
Tick-tock, tick-tock, the clocks all conspire,
To create a riddle wrapped in desire.

Painted smiles on potato-shaped friends,
Whisper secrets where nonsense transcends.
Who knew that a tomato could feel so spry?
In this gallery, the absurd can fly.

So gaze at the portraits we all create,
Each brushstroke, a laugh, each hue, a fate.
For life's strange tapestry, let's weave with delight,
In the gallery of quirks, let's dance through the night.

The Silence Between Beats

In the pause of the clock, there's a giggle,
Time winks at us, oh what a riddle.
We chase after seconds, like cats on a wall,
Only to find we've been jesters for all.

With laughter, we dance in the gaps of our days,
Like clowns at a fair, lost in whimsical ways.
A hiccup in heartbeat, a blunder of fate,
We swirl through the silence; it's never too late.

Whispers of Forgotten Truths

Oh, the whispers that tickle the back of our mind,
Like lost sock companions, so hard to find.
With truths wrapped in bubbles, we float through our years,
As silly as penguins, we giggle through tears.

The universe nudges, a wink in its tone,
As we ponder all secrets we've somehow outgrown.
We scribble on napkins, make plans for the world,
While secrets keep dancing, like flags all unfurled.

The Secrets We Hold in Silence

In the hush of our hearts, secrets tumble and roll,
Like marbles in pockets, they dance and console.
With a chuckle we ponder the things we won't say,
Pretending life's like a game we all play.

Umbrellas of wisdom, we hold them askew,
As rain falls on thoughts that we keep hidden too.
Oh, the jokes that we cradle beneath our straight faces,
Life's a riddle we juggle in curious places.

Navigating the Ocean of Thoughts

With a compass of whimsy, we set sail today,
Through waves of confusion, we giggle and play.
A surfboard of musings, we ride and we fall,
As seagulls of insight laugh over it all.

We fish for the answers in a sea made of dreams,
Reeling in nonsense, or so it seems.
But each splash of our laughter is gold in disguise,
In this ocean of thought, we're all the wise guys.

Forgotten Poems of the Soul

In the depths of our mind's jumbled space,
Lies a muse who forgot how to race.
She scribbles in margins, all crossed out,
A riddle of socks, what is life about?

A cat wearing glasses lounges all day,
Chasing red dots that just fade away.
The fish in the bowl rolls his big, round eyes,
As the dog ponders truths in a world full of lies.

With each silly giggle and query we make,
We stumble through reasons like a tumbleweed shake.
Our wisdom wrapped up in a chocolate treat,
Is life just dessert? Oh, isn't that sweet?

So laugh and embrace the quirks that we find,
For in chaos and wonder, we're all intertwined.
A dance in the kitchen, a wink from the moon,
Life's a playful jaunt, a comical tune.

Sifting Through Eternity

In the grand cosmic joke, we pick out the stars,
While juggling our dreams, and playing guitars.
A unicorn sneezes, rainbows take flight,
As we ponder our purpose in the still of the night.

The crumbs of existence all scattered around,
Reveal answers hiding in laughter's sound.
A sock puppet thinks he's a wise old sage,
As we flip through pages of life's funny stage.

Flip-flops on cats do a curious jig,
While life's greatest truths dance like a twig.
We chase after meaning like kids in a game,
And it seems every time, we're never the same.

So mix up your laughter with a dash of delight,
Converse with your coffee from morning till night.
In the joyous absurdity, just take a seat,
For the search for the truth is quite the silly feat.

Lanterns in the Dark

In shadows where we trip and fall,
We light our path with laughter's call.
A wink, a grin, a cosmic jest,
Who knew confusion could feel the best?

With every question, our brains ignite,
Why did the chicken cross the night?
To find what's lost in plain old sight,
Or just to show us there's no fright?

The stars above, they blink and giggle,
As we all scramble, trying to wiggle.
In puzzling mess, joy starts to bloom,
Like socks that vanish, from the room!

So let's embrace this charming mess,
Life's riddle wrapped in a comfy dress.
With lanterns bright, we'll joke and play,
And dance through night to greet the day.

Unraveling Time's Fabric

Tick-tock, the clock has lost its grace,
A time warp dance, oh what a race!
Yesterday's news is today's delight,
Did a cat just steal my lunch tonight?

History's taught us how to blend,
But why do old trends always offend?
That bell-bottom phase, did it really fit?
Or was it just our minds taking a hit?

In this patchwork quilt of past and now,
We stitch our choices—wait, what, how?
A knitting needle from future's hand,
Creates a sweater that no one planned.

So grab your yarn, and twist it tight,
We'll laugh at time, it's quite the sight!
For every moment that slips away,
We'll wear our whims like hats at play.

Echoes of Abandonment

In the attic of forgotten dreams,
Dusty toys spin with moonlight beams.
A teddy bear whispers secrets old,
While mismatched socks sit, stories untold.

We often leave our hopes behind,
Chasing whims, a rare and kind.
A rubber duck sings a lonely tune,
While echoes giggle beneath the moon.

The echoes call us back to play,
In the land of once-upon-a-day.
A game of peek-a-boo with fate,
Will make us grin before it's late.

So gather up what's left behind,
Rediscover all the joy we find.
In these echoes, laughter runs deep,
Like sleepy dreams, we just might keep.

Hymns of Humanity

We humans march with clumsy grace,
Stumbling through a magical place.
With hearts aglow, we mime and sway,
In the grand ballet of the everyday.

From coffee spills to epic fails,
Our epic tales spin like dandelion tales.
With every laugh, a note is sung,
In this odd choir, we're all just young.

The quirks we share, a unified show,
Like socks that vanish, but let's not go!
For in our chaos, we find the rhyme,
An awkward dance through a just-in-time.

So let us sing, oh joyful crowd,
For every mishap leads to the loud.
In humanity's hymn, we find delight,
As we all stumble toward the light.

The Weight of Shadows

Shadows dance on the wall, so spry,
As the sun says goodbye and the stars get shy.
Do they weigh us down or help us to play?
I trip over sighs in the dwindling day.

They whisper secrets, oh so profound,
While I'm just here making goofy sounds.
Like a shadow confused by the bright afternoon,
I question my purpose, I'm lost like a balloon.

Do they hide our mischief or show us our flaws?
Maybe they're jesters with invisible claws.
I laugh at their antics, absurd yet amusing,
In the theater of life where I'm merely cruising.

So let shadows tease and tickle my soul,
For in their deep depths, we all play a role.
A giggle amidst ponderings, wild and surreal,
Perhaps they're just here for the comic appeal.

Seasons Shifting in Silence

Winter wears socks that don't match, oh dear,
While summer is sunbathing with no sense of fear.
Spring's busy sneezing, the flowers aflame,
And autumn's a hoarder, it's losing the game.

Leaves fall like confetti, a colorful mess,
Each season, confused, seems to harbor some stress.
Rain dances with sunshine, a cha-cha they prance,
In this four-act play, life takes quite the chance.

Yet here I stand, sipping tea with a grin,
While the seasons debate what's lost and what's win.
Do they ponder their purpose, or just change the scene?
I can't help but chuckle at their little routine.

With seasons shifting in a comical race,
I'm wondering if we should all join the chase.
For in this warm chaos, we grow and we fumble,
Creating our own little stumbles and grumbles.

Legacies Unwritten

Ink spills with giggles on pages of fate,
While I scribble my thoughts on the edge of a plate.
Should I draft a grand novel, or stick with a meme?
In the book of my life, what's the ultimate theme?

Each legacy whispers, 'Don't be such a bore!'
As I trip on my words, tumble into folklore.
Confessions of cheese, or a recipe with flair,
Who's gonna care? It's all just hot air.

My future's a canvas of wild, crazy strokes,
Filled with laughter and possibly some jokes.
So I raise up my coffee, toast lofty ideals,
To legacies unwritten, let's see how it feels!

And when the last chapter comes, full of delight,
I'll smile through the chaos, it's all out of sight.
With doodles and jests, my spirit won't fade,
A legacy captured—a cosmic charade!

Cracks in the Facade

The world wears a mask that's cracked and askew,
With smiles painted bright, but the humor is few.
Behind every chuckle, a giggle might hide,
In the cracks of the facade, where laughter has cried.

Life's a comedy club with a jester's blunder,
Where dreams drift like balloons in the skies of wonder.
We juggle our worries, while slipping on ice,
In this circus of chaos, there's never a price.

Punchlines are hidden in everyday scenes,
Where the absurd collides with the in-betweens.
I wink at the cracks, they mirror my fears,
For laughter's the language that brightens our years.

So let's break the facade, let the ridicule flow,
With joy in our hearts, we'll put on a show.
In the theater of nonsense, let's dance through the night,
For amidst all the chaos, there's humor in sight.

Cartography of the Unknown

In skies of blue, they chart their maps,
Where X marks spots like funny naps.
With squirrels as guides, they roam and play,
Finding lost socks along the way.

The sea of socks, a treasure vast,
I found my shoe, but where'd it pass?
With compasses wild and laughter loud,
They sail through life, a playful crowd.

They sketch out roads on candy lanes,
And laugh at routes through puddles' plains.
In every turn and quirky twist,
A fortune cookie could not resist.

Yet through the chaos, wisdom calls,
It's not the path, but how one falls.
So grab your map, and join the fun,
Life's a journey, not a run.

Conversations with Time

Tick-tock, the clock just chimed,
It winked at me, and I just rhymed.
With seconds dancing, minutes tease,
They steal my snack like favorite cheese.

I asked old Time, 'Where do you go?'
He laughed and said, 'You'll never know!'
Through coffee spills and silly pranks,
He skips along, our funny banks.

With calendars filled with doodles bright,
We plot our days with pure delight.
In chatty whispers, it unfolds,
Each tick a story, laugh it holds.

So grab a moment, hold it tight,
For time's a jester, full of light.
Life's a circus, a comedy show,
In every tick, let laughter grow.

Kaleidoscope of Dreams

Through swirling colors, dreams collide,
A chubby cat takes us for a ride.
In jellybean skies, we dance around,
With gummy bears, they make no sound.

Each twist we take, a new surprise,
With cotton candy clouds that rise.
"Let's bake a cake from dreams," I said,
And off we soared, to sugar-fred.

In twisting tunnels of bright delight,
Where marshmallows giggle through the night.
With ice cream rivers, we float on by,
While rainbow fish jump and fly.

A kaleidoscope spins, a sight to see,
With laughs and glimmers, wild and free.
So take a dip in colors bright,
And live each dream, it's pure delight.

Lost in the Labyrinth of Thought

In a maze of thoughts, I took a turn,
Where light bulbs flash, and ideas burn.
A hedgehog led me with a grin,
"How do we start? Where do we begin?"

Through walls of whimsy, I wander deep,
Chasing shadows, counting sheep.
A thought balloon popped with such great flair,
It showered me with dreams to wear.

I met a gnome who danced with glee,
He juggled answers, one, two, three.
"Why not venture into the absurd,
Where nonsense and giggles are often stirred?"

So in this labyrinth, let's lose our way,
With every question, let's laugh and play.
For in the twists, both odd and fun,
Life's a riddle where we all run.

The Compass of the Heart

In the map of our days, we seek a sign,
Lost in laughter, where the sun does shine.
With a compass that spins, we chase our dreams,
Maybe it's coffee, or so it seems.

When life gives you lemons, make a bright pie,
Or maybe a lemonade that gets you high.
In this quest for joy, we trip and fall,
But hey, that's just dancing at the next ball.

Some say it's love, and others say cats,
A mix of good food and occasional spats.
Yet here we are, with our quirks all around,
Finding treasure in moments, blissfully unbound.

Nature's Enigmatic Song

Birds chirp in verses, trees hum along,
A melody plays, both goofy and strong.
The squirrels hold concerts, acorns the stage,
While crickets compose from their cozy cage.

The wind whispers secrets, though hard to catch,
Like a riddle from nature with no clear match.
Do ants have a rhythm, or is it a dance?
We ponder, we chuckle, always in trance.

So let's sing with frogs, who croak life's refrain,
While rainbows and puddles let joy entertain.
The world's a grand symphony, funny and bright,
And we're just the notes, dancing in delight.

Reflections in the Starlit Sky

Stars are but sparkles on a black velvet dress,
Winking and giggling, causing such mess.
We ponder their purpose, all twinkling bright,
"Do they know our secrets?" we muse in the night.

In the silence of space, even comets can laugh,
As they zip through the cosmos, a comical path.
The moon gives a wink, "Oh, it's just a phase,"
While we earthlings wonder in silly amaze.

With telescopes ready, we search for delight,
But all we find are aliens, hosting a fight.
So let's join the laughter in this starry show,
For mysteries are answered with each gleaming glow.

Questions Written in Stardust

In the cosmos, questions float on a breeze,

Like socks in the laundry, lost without keys.

"Is our fate in a cookie or scribbled in stars?"

We laugh at the thought, while driving our cars.

Why do ducks quack and machines just beep?

Are dreams what we chase, or naps that we keep?

Each query a giggle, each ponder a jest,

The truth feels much lighter when we're at our best.

So we scribble our thoughts on the back of a napkin,

Seeking the answers with each little tapping.

In the dance of existence, we're humorously tossed,

Finding joy in the questions, never too lost.

Gravity of Dreams

In dreams, we fly like clumsy bats,
Chasing cheese that talks and chats.
The laws of gravity just take a break,
While we debate if cheese can shake.

Jumping high to touch the stars,
Accidentally crashing into cars.
Life is silly, so let's not frown,
Just don't wear pajamas in the town.

We toss our worries into the wind,
Where logic and reason surely rescind.
Finding joy in absurdity's grace,
Embracing chaos, a smiling face.

For dreams can land us anywhere,
In a world where penguins wear a chair.
So laugh out loud, let spirits gleam,
For life is stranger than our wildest dream.

Tokens from Yesterday

A sock from childhood, full of holes,
It carries memories, laughter, and shoals.
Tickle fights and jelly stains,
In the attic, nostalgia reigns.

Photographs with goofy grins,
Remind us of our epic wins.
From awkward dances in school halls,
To daring feats at the neighborhood walls.

Collecting tokens like a squirrel's hoard,
But not all of them are adored.
Some things are best left in the past,
Like that haircut—how long will it last?

So treasure those moments, both weird and sweet,
As you dance through time on tangled feet.
For yesterday's tokens laugh with you,
As they whisper secrets of all you knew.

The Road Less Traveled

Two paths ahead, both seem absurd,
One's filled with sand, the other's a bird.
Let's flip a coin, toss it up high,
And see where fate leads this curious guy.

I stumbled on rocks, kicked up some dust,
And tried to read signs, oh goodness, I must.
That road had laughter, and puddles to splash,
Where squirrels would gossip and make quite a bash.

With a left turn and a foolish grin,
I found a dance floor where I could spin.
Bumping into joy, I leapt and I twirled,
Life's a big party, let's see how it's swirled!

So here's to the choices, silly and bright,
To roads less traveled, filled with delight.
With friends by our side and snacks for the ride,
We'll wander together, all worries aside.

Threads of Connection

We're all just threads in a silly loom,
Stitched together to dance and bloom.
From knitting groups to chatty cafes,
Life's a patchwork of colorful frays.

A yarn that tangles, unravels in fun,
As we twist and turn under the sun.
With laughter, we tie our stories tight,
Creating a tapestry, a joy-filled sight.

So grab a string and add your flair,
Don't mind the knots, we'll all share.
For every stitch we weave is bold,
In this comedy of life, we're all retold.

Let's celebrate the quirks we hold,
In this thread of connection, bright and bold.
So pick up your needles, give it a spin,
Together, we'll laugh, let the stitching begin!

Fragments of Infinity

In a world full of choices, we roam,
Like a cat chasing shadows, far from home.
Chasing cosmic dust with a fork and a knife,
Wondering if this is the essence of life.

We dance with our socks on, mismatched in pairs,
Baking cookies while avoiding our cares.
With sprinkles of chaos, we laugh at the strife,
Embracing the madness, oh what a life!

Our dreams are like bubbles that float through the air,
Pop them with laughter, that's the way we dare.
In this circus of moments, we juggle and strive,
Finding joy in the quirks that help us survive.

So let's toast to the questions, sip tea in the dark,
Like fireflies dancing, we'll find our spark.
Through giggles and mishaps, let's cherish the ride,
For in every small moment, the fun can't be denied.

Echoes of Existence

We wander through life with cereal for brains,
In a quest for the meaning while dodging the rains.
Are we tiny ants or grand cosmic whales?
Perhaps we're just cats, with fantastical tales!

With every odd mishap, we scratch our heads,
Are we meant to thrive or sleep in our beds?
Jumping to conclusions, oh what a delight,
Life's punchlines are waiting, morning till night.

We scribble on napkins, make sense of the mess,
Examining chaos, we wear it like dress.
With laughter as our guide, we chuckle and spin,
Finding treasures in chaos, let the fun begin!

So let's laugh at the puzzle, it's quirky and bright,
With hiccups and giggles, we'll guide our own flight.
In this grand circus of being, let's relish and play,
For the echoes of existence are here to stay.

Unspoken Truths of the Heart

Beneath the surface, we hide our true face,
Like socks in the dryer, lost in the race.
What makes us tick? A sandwich? A tease?
Like kids on the playground, we laugh with such ease.

With our hearts in our hands, we juggle our dreams,
Like ice cream sundaes melting at the seams.
We speak in riddles and giggles and sighs,
Unearthing the truths, like a child's big eyes.

In moments of silence, we throw in some cheer,
With planets and pancakes, we conquer our fear.
We leap through the dark, with a skip and a beat,
Finding joy in the chaos that makes us complete.

So let's dance in the rain while the world spins around,
With laughs as our music, let's make joyful sound.
In the playful embrace of the quirky and smart,
We cherish the secrets of the unspoken heart.

Veils of Reality

With veils made of laughter, we twirl and we spin,
In the carnival of life, let the fun begin!
Are we ghosts of the past or stars of the show?
In this wacky adventure, who truly will know?

We dream of big dreams, in pajamas and socks,
Building castles of pillows and making grand knocks.
Are we warriors of whimsy or jesters of fate?
We dance with the absurd, and oh how we relate!

Through time's silly prism, we glance and we peek,
With giggles and grins, let's embrace the unique.
A riddle, a joke in the cosmic design,
In the chaos of living, we discover the fine.

So let's raise our glasses to the quirky and strange,
In this circus of life, let's boldly exchange.
With humor our compass, we'll navigate right,
For the veils of our reality lead to pure delight.

Unfolding the Enigma

Why do socks disappear when washed?
Are they off to a world that's posh?
Do they mingle, dance, and dine?
Or just hide where the old shoes recline?

Why do cats stare at nothing in air?
Plotting schemes with a devious glare?
Is the universe full of mice?
Or just a world where they roll the dice?

Should cereal float or should it sink?
How about dishes that wash in a blink?
Do we ponder things and just miff?
Or just enjoy the big cosmic riff?

When do we laugh and when do we cry?
Is it saved for the moments we try?
Life's a puzzle with pieces amiss,
But sometimes it's just about bliss.

Chronicles of the Unexplained

Why do dreams play tricks on our minds?
One day dragon, the next a fountain of pine,
Do they whisper secrets or just giggle?
Life's a riddle—just take a wiggle.

Why do we misplace our keys all the time?
Are they off dancing, in rhythm, in rhyme?
Maybe they found a good local bar,
Sipping tea with a sentient car?

Do plants have a chat while we sleep?
Discussing why we dare not leap?
Or do they mock when we water too late?
"Look at that human, it's all second-rate!"

What's with the ice cream that melts so fast?
A sweet moment gone, never meant to last?
Life's a cone with a slippery side,
Hold on tight, enjoy the ride!

Afoot on the Path

Where's the map for this give-and-take?
They hand you lessons but not a mistake,
Is there a handbook for juggling life?
Or just skill in avoiding the strife?

What's with the cat that always meows?
Is he running a club with the local cows?
Maybe they're planning a secret parade,
While dashing off to the marmalade?

Do butterflies think about what they'll wear?
Flapping freely without a care?
Life's a wardrobe of colors, it seems,
Twirl around like you're living in dreams.

Can you play hopscotch on clouds of blue?
Can dreams swirl and dance beneath the dew?
Life's an odd game with marbles and tricks,
Just remember, it's all in the mix!

Whimsies of Wonder

Why do we chuckle at dad jokes so loud?
Do they tickle the wisdom of the proud?
Or is it just laughter for laughing's own sake?
Giggles abound with each faux pas to make?

Why does the toast land butter-side down?
Is there a reason for this comical frown?
Maybe it's fate sharing a wink,
Or just a twist of the universe's link?

Why do we ponder the stars up so high?
Are they hiding answers or just passing by?
Or is it a game where we flip and dive,
Chasing wonders that help us survive?

Life's a circus with wonders galore,
Juggling moments, forever in store,
So laugh a little, and snicker with glee,
For life's a puzzle, come join the spree!

Treasures Beneath the Surface

Beneath the waves where secrets hide,
A rubber ducky floats with pride.
It whispers tales of sunken ships,
And golden coins that swim in dips.

The treasure map is scribbled out,
In crayon crumpled, full of doubt.
The X marks spots where dreams collide,
Unraveling laughter in the tide.

Each crab a sage, with sideways dance,
Mocks the goldfish's little chance.
In seaweed debates, they all convene,
To solve why humans can't swim keen.

They giggle as the gulls squawk loud,
Chasing rainbows in a feathered crowd.
For truth is buried, yonder so,
In bubbles of fun where glee will flow.

Reflections of an Infinite Journey

On a road less traveled, funny signs,
Point directions lost in yarn designs.
The map is old and slightly torn,
Yet laughter thrives, and frowns are shorn.

Each turn unveils a wacky view,
With dancing trees and skies so blue.
A talking turtle, wise and sage,
Recites the nonsense of a vintage age.

Who knew a cow could play guitar?
It serenades beneath a star.
In every pit stop, joy does bloom,
As laughter chases away the gloom.

So travel far and travel wide,
With giggles riding by your side.
For each reflection brings a jest,
In every heart, there lies a quest.

Whispers in the Cosmos

Stars blink down with a cheeky grin,
Wondering where our thoughts have been.
Comets tailing in goofy haste,
Chasing each other in cosmic waste.

The planets spin in a dizzy dance,
Each takes a turn in a merry chance.
While aliens sip their cosmic tea,
Sharing the gossip of you and me.

Black holes are just the universe's vacuum,
Sucking in all the lost costume gloom.
With glitter dust from supernovae,
They sparkled like it's a Broadway soirée.

So when you gaze at that nightly sight,
Remember it's all a playful light.
The cosmos chuckles with each twist,
As dreams float off in a starry mist.

Shadows of Eternal Questions

In corners dark where giggles grow,
Shadows question, 'What do we know?'
A cat with a hat ponders deep,
While aiming for a cloud to leap.

Why do socks disappear in dryers?
Do toaster crumbs play as liars?
These ponderings swirl and flip like pies,
With every glance, a new surprise.

A cactus winks with prickly jest,
And ruminates on life's behest.
Why do humans sit and stare?
When laughter's the answer everywhere!

So dance with shadows, when they appear,
For in their giggles lies no fear.
Questions resonant in silly tones,
Crafting wisdom in joyful groans.

Beneath the Surface of Dream

In a world where ducks wear hats,
And pineapples play piano,
We ponder all the juicy facts,
While sipping on our avocado.

Questions float on fluffy clouds,
Like popcorn at a movie night,
We laugh at dreams in silly shrouds,
As shadows dance in soft moonlight.

A turtle tells a knock-knock joke,
While fireflies join in the fun,
We giggle at the words we spoke,
As the laugh track comes undone.

But what if life's a kooky show?
With punchlines hidden in plain sight,
We just go with the flow,
And belly laugh into the night.

Love Letters to the Universe

Dear Universe, you sly old fox,
You wrapped my cat in silver spark,
I sent my love in rhythm blocks,
But you just left me in the dark.

Starry winks from distant gleams,
Followed by a comet's sigh,
You scribbled back in cosmic dreams,
And sent my heart into the sky.

The moon rolled over, tossed a wink,
While planets laughed in circles tight,
Oh, tell me more—do you think?
Is love just gravity in flight?

I'll write again, dear cosmic friend,
With jellybeans and cotton candy,
And promise not to ever end,
This funny dance, so sweet and dandy.

The Heartbeat of Mystery

A penguin wears a polka dot tie,
And dances with a waving fish,
What's lurking in the blueberry pie?
A secret recipe? A wish?

Tick tock, the clock just did a spin,
While rabbits held a card parade,
The heartbeat of the world begins,
With jokes that linger, never fade.

Why do socks vanish in the wash?
Is there a party in the machine?
With turtle soup and marshmallows posh,
A riddle's answer — seldom seen.

But isn't that the joy of life?
To chuckle while we twist and twirl,
Chasing dreams without any strife,
As mystery gives laughter a swirl.

Smiles in the Dark

In shadows where the giggles bloom,
A chocolate cake begins to sing,
It spins and swirls within the room,
As moonlight tickles everything.

A pair of shoes start tap-dancing,
While beans in pots begin to chat,
The night brings forth its wild prancing,
And whispers secrets — imagine that!

Laughter echoes off the walls,
As stars drop in for a soiree,
With popcorn flying through the halls,
Each smile a glimpse of bright ballet.

So if you find yourself alone,
In darkness, think of silly rhymes,
For joy will make each heart a stone,
And lift us up with jolly chimes.

Silhouettes of Understanding

In a park where pigeons plot,
I asked a squirrel, what have you got?
He scratched his head and said with flair,
"Just some nuts and a dash of air!"

A wise old tree, with bark so rough,
Grumbled softly, "Life is just tough.
But swing with joy on a bouncy swing,
You'll find the joy in simple things!"

A cloud passed by, in cotton candy,
And whispered, "Life's a bit dandy!
Dance with shadows; laugh and grin,
For the wittiest tales live within!"

So here we are, in playful jest,
Chasing questions, never at rest.
With each small laugh and pondering flight,
We uncover truths wrapped up in light!

Quest for the Unseen

With a map that leads to nowhere fast,
I tripped through time, oh what a blast!
A chicken crossed my path and laughed,
"Seek fortune now, not the photograph!"

Lost in thoughts, my eyes were wide,
While searching for gifts that the stars may hide.
A frog croaked loudly, mischief in play,
"Jump right in; see life our way!"

An old magician with cards in hand,
Tried to teach me a trick so grand.
He said, "To find the truth out here,
Just watch the world and hold what's dear!"

Through winding trails and silly cries,
Life is more than suits and ties.
So grab a friend, off on your quest,
The unseen joy is life's finest jest!

Chronicles of the Soul

My cat once told me, with a yawn,
"Life's a tale that's never drawn.
Chase the sun, ignore the night,
For naps are the key to delight!"

A silly owl with glasses on,
Said, "Worry not about what's gone.
Just hoot away when fate's unkind,
And watch how laughter soothes the mind!"

A fish in a bowl, wearing a crown,
Proclaimed, "Life's a show, don't wear a frown!
Swim with flair, let troubles unfold,
The true gold lies in the stories told!"

So through these tales of plain antics,
We find bright colors in life's antics.
Dance with whimsy, float on a roll,
For every heartbeat's a tale for the soul!

Mirrors of Fate

In the mirror, a grin I found,
It winked back as I spun around.
"Life's just a dance, don't miss the beat,
Join the parade with silly feet!"

A jester's hat sat atop my head,
As I juggled thoughts, feeling misled.
"Castles of doubt? Just made of sand,
Watch them fall, isn't life so grand?"

The moonlight laughed, a brilliant tease,
"Stand upright, sway gently in the breeze.
For choices made on a whim or two,
Reveal the art that lives in you!"

So here's a toast, with a hiccup or two,
To the quirks and giggles life throws at you.
In every reflection, be proud and state,
The joy of being is the best fate!

Whispers of Existence

In a universe so vast and wide,
We ponder purpose with comical pride.
Is it tacos or nachos that bring us cheer?
Or just the chance to guzzle cold beer?

Stars twinkle bright, but do they even know?
If we're just dust, why put on a show?
Life's quirks are plenty, like a cat with a hat,
Chasing its tail while we all just gasp at that!

Between cosmic wonders and sock puppets' glee,
What's truly profound? A joke from a tree?
The orbs may spin, but we trip on our laces,
Finding the absurd in all of life's races.

So grab a rubber chicken, let laughter ignite,
As we skip through the cosmos, all day and all night.
Existence is wacky, a circus all right,
Swinging from joy to the occasional fright!

Unraveling the Cosmic Thread

In a world of chaos, we weave our fate,
Are we lost in the fabric, or just fashionably late?
With every twist and turn, we chuckle and sigh,
Wondering if the sky has a leftover pie.

Wormholes and quarks, what a tangled mess!
Yet, here we are, trying to impress.
Life's grand tapestry has lost all its flair,
When we can't find our socks in the cosmic air.

Chasing our tails like a dog at the park,
Unraveling threads 'til we trip on a spark.
Are we just jokes in a divine stand-up act?
Or fuzzy musings on a galactic contract?

So dance with the quirks, embrace the absurd,
As we laugh at the jokes that bullets never heard.
With a wink to the cosmos, we strut and we sway,
In this beautiful mess, we'll find our own way.

Echoes in the Void

In the silence of space, can you hear me shout?
While juggling our dreams, we still have our doubts.
Galaxies spinning, but what's that they say?
"Your socks are out there, just drifting away!"

Stars may be bright, but who lights the way?
Is it cosmic confetti from a stellar buffet?
Between black holes and laughs that we echo,
There's cake in the fridge! Don't forget to go!

Gravity pulls us with a comedic grace,
As we float through the void, all over the place.
Do we hear the laughter of cosmic comedians?
Or just the sound of our snacks at the median?

Existence is tricky, a punchline divine,
Splitting our sides over coffee and wine.
So here in the void, let us kick back and play,
Embrace the absurd on this wild, wacky day!

A Dance with Destiny

Life's a dance, with two left feet,
With missed steps and trips, we still feel the beat.
Destiny giggles as we swirl and sway,
Trying to keep rhythm, but end up in dismay.

With every wrong turn, the universe grins,
As we find joy in the chaos and whims.
Is it fate or a prank from a cosmic clown?
When your partner's a chicken in a goofy brown gown?

So waltz through the wonders, foxtrot through strife,
With a twirl and a chuckle, let's dance through this life.
With each wobbly move and a jest from the stars,
We may trip on our dreams, but they're never too far.

So here's to the missteps, the laughter, the fun,
Embrace every moment; we've only just begun.
For in this grand ball with all its surprise,
We'll shimmy through stardust, alive in our eyes!

The Silence Between Moments

In the quiet, thoughts all stray,
What's for dinner? Or a play?
Did I leave the stove on high?
Or is that just my inner sigh?

Counting socks, a favorite sport,
Where did that missing one abort?
Time takes twists like a wild vine,
I'll label each thought, just to shine!

Do trees judge us when we trip?
And do clouds gossip on their trip?
We ponder life while chasing bees,
With laughter caught in summer's breeze.

So raise a toast, let silliness thrive,
In this circus, we can survive!
Laugh through puzzles, twist and twine,
For in confusion, we're just fine!

Pulse of the Universe

Stars blinking like they know a joke,
Is that a whisper or just smoke?
Galaxies dance in cosmic flair,
While I search for my lost hair!

Planets spin with a wobbly grin,
Do they know where we fit in?
Aliens chuckle at our fears,
Counting their laughs through the years.

Black holes gobbling up our snacks,
Do they share, or simply relax?
Each comet brings a silly tale,
A cosmic ship on a wild sail.

So here's to space and its big heart,
Each twinkle plays a funny part!
In the vastness, we find our tune,
Like dancing ants beneath the moon.

Reflections in a Raindrop

Each droplet holds a world so bright,
A park bench chat in the twilight.
Do raindrops giggle as they fall?
I'd ask, but they won't recall!

Puddles mirror my silly face,
With squishy shoes, I join the race.
Nature sings a wet refrain,
While I ponder who's to blame!

An umbrella's turned like a wild hat,
Can it tell jokes? I think not that!
Water's dancing on my nose,
As I discover mystery's prose.

So splash about, when skies are gray,
Life's a puddle, let's swim and play!
With laughter floating, drop by drop,
In the rain, we'll never stop!

Dreamscapes of Thought

In dreams, my cat can sing and fly,
A napkin talks, oh my, oh my!
Balloons debate why they float,
While a lamp post writes a note.

Chasing cheese in a field of hair,
Finding socks with a flair and care.
Do jerks in dreams applaud my style?
Or do they frown and walk a mile?

Slipping gardens, turtle races,
Each dream grants us funny faces.
Whispering wishes on the breeze,
Searching truth among the leaves.

So let's awake with giggles shared,
In our dreams, we never cared!
Life's a dance, absurd yet sweet,
With daydreams where the silly meet!

Celestial Conversations

Stars gather close, with twinkling eyes,
They chat about how, we rise and rise.
"Why count your socks? What's the deal?"
"Just wear mismatched, it's a celestial feel!"

Aliens ponder, with a giggle or two,
"Do they really think they are just passing through?"
They take a sip of cosmic tea,
And laugh at our woes, as if they were free.

Journey Beyond the Ordinary

A snail with a hat, he dreams of the stars,
While leaping frogs talk of marzipan bars.
"Why scurry to deadlines!" the turtle shouts loud,
"I'll take it slow, and make my own crowd!"

A cat with a tie, reads books made of cheese,
While squirrels debate if they'll conquer the breeze.
"Worry is wasteful," the wise owl does chime,
"Let's dance like the flowers, and giggle in rhyme!"

Enigma of the Everyday

Why do toast slices always land face down?
Is it fate, or the crumbs of the town?
The coffee pot sighs, as it brews with finesse,
While mugs whisper gossip, with playful excess!

The doorbell rings, does it sing to the moon?
Or is it just boredom, that makes it a tune?
Each chore is a riddle, like socks in the wash,
The mystery deepens, as we all take a posh!

Threads of Destiny

Life's a blanket stitched with strange threads,
Some are rainbow, others are reds.
"Why call it fate?" the goldfish does grin,
"Just make your own wishes, and dive right in!"

A statue of cheese dreams of brie on the moon,
As teapots debate how to better their tune.
"Confessions of spoons," they declare with a twist,
Life's just a party, you get what you wish!

Living in the Margins

In the margins, scribbles dance,
A lost sock caught in life's prance.
Coffee spills on my grand design,
Yet here I laugh, and feel just fine.

Lunch breaks turn to life advice,
Like pancakes tossed with some spice.
We scribble notes on napkin dreams,
Finding clarity in messy themes.

Who needs a map, or grand debate?
I'll take the road where ducks await.
With rubber ducks and silly hats,
I'll ponder life's mysterious chats.

So if you see my typo'd fate,
Just wave and smile, let's celebrate.
For in the quirks, and all that's strange,
We find the fun in every change.

Weaving Through the Chaos

Tangled threads in bright array,
I pull at knots that won't obey.
A tapestry of hopes and fears,
I laugh at yarn that disappears.

Spaghetti nights and wine poured free,
I wonder if that's just for me.
Knitting wisdom, instead of clothes,
I pen my thoughts, where no one knows.

Life's a dance, and I'm offbeat,
With mismatched socks, I find my seat.
In every twist, a laugh, a grin,
The chaos blooms, let's all jump in!

So grab a thread or roll of tape,
We'll stitch the seams and mend escape.
For in the mess of who we are,
We weave our dreams, a shining star.

The Flicker of Tomorrow

Tomorrow's light peeks through the door,
I trip on shoelaces, then explore.
With coffee spills and playful grins,
I chase the day and all its whims.

A rubber chicken, that's the key,
To understanding the mystery.
It squeaks and honks, it flaps about,
Reminds me life's a silly shout.

So if you see me dance in rain,
With puddles as my cheerful stage,
I'll twirl and leap, a child's delight,
In every moment, pure and bright.

Tomorrow's flicker, it will shine,
As I embrace the subtle sign.
For in the joy that life bestows,
A dance of dreams forever grows.

Dialogue of the Heart

My heart takes notes, it writes a play,
With funny lines that stray away.
It whispers secrets heard by few,
With giggles shared and bright, bold hues.

In silly voices, we partake,
A chocolate cake, or two to bake.
With every laugh, it learns to sing,
And opens up the quirkiest spring.

So let's chat deep, with latte in hand,
About the world and dreams so grand.
With every sip, we'll toss our fears,
And find connection through our cheers.

In this dialogue, we find our role,
A blend of humor, heart, and soul.
For in the quirks of who we are,
We paint our lives, a winking star.

Beneath the Surface of Being

Beneath the waves of daily grind,
Lurks a squid with jokes so blind,
He juggles dreams and extra fries,
While reminding us we're wise to try.

Life's but a sandwich on a plate,
With pickles in a pickle state,
We munch on thoughts of what it means,
As mustard spills our hopes and dreams.

Between the chores and coffee breaks,
A punchline hides, our laughter wakes,
The universe, a big clown's nose,
With every whim, the cosmos glows.

So grab a snack and take a seat,
Let whimsy guide your tired feet,
For underneath the serious stuff,
The universe just wants to puff.

Shadows of the Unseen

In shadows where the lost socks dwell,
A secret lives, but who can tell?
It's here among the dusty things,
That laughter blooms and madness sings.

The lights go dim, the jokes take flight,
As unseen shadows plan a fright,
They dance and jiggle, and in a whirl,
Both chickens and the wisdom twirl.

What's deeper than the couch we sink?
Is it wisdom, or just a drink?
In echoes where the silence laughs,
Life's greatest puzzle hides in halves.

So next time when you meet the void,
Remember, laughter can't be toyed,
For in the dark, hilarity reigns,
And shadows come with silly chains.

Chasing Fleeting Illusions

Like bubblegum on summer's day,
Illusions pop and drift away,
We chase them down with open hearts,
Only to find they're just strange parts.

A jumping bean with legs up high,
Claims it's the reason earth meets sky,
But when you stoop to catch that dream,
It fizzles out—a silly gleam.

Fleeting joys just play the game,
With laughter, they ignite the flame,
A rubber chicken in disguise,
Reminds us laughter never dies.

So waltz along this merry path,
With every giggle, add to math,
For what we chase and hold so tight,
Are just the winks of pure delight.

Threads of Time and Wonder

Across the loom of tangled fate,
Threads of purple, gold, and eight,
We weave our hopes with bits of lace,
And wonder why we raced this race.

Time ticks on with shoes untied,
While serendipity takes a ride,
It skips and hops through tangled hair,
A cosmic joke that's ever rare.

Through doodles drawn on paper backs,
In crayon scents, life builds its tracks,
With every scribble, joy takes flight,
As meaning hides in kid's delight.

So thread your needle, sew a dream,
Let laughter burst from every seam,
For in each stitch, we find our cheer,
In fabric's weave, the truth is clear.

The Dance of Paradox

In life's grand ball, we twirl with glee,
But where's the exit? Can't you see?
We laugh at choices, both big and small,
Waltzing through chaos, we trip and fall.

With every step, we chase and flee,
Tickled by answers, lost at sea.
The more we question, the less we find,
In this silly game of the curious mind.

We juggle tasks, a circus act,
While wearing mismatched socks, that's a fact.
Each riddle solved, another appears,
Like socks in the wash, they disappear!

So let us dance on this quirky floor,
Embracing absurdity, who could ask for more?
With humor as our guiding star,
We'll waltz through life, no matter how bizarre.

Navigating the Unknown

Maps are for wimps, let's take a stroll,
Into the wilderness, that's my goal!
With a compass spinning like a whirling dervish,
I wander aimlessly, oh, how I relish!

Questions flutter like butterflies, bright,
Each one a riddle that sparks delight.
We seek the truth, but it's lost in the fray,
Like socks that vanish, day after day.

I ask the stars, they're silent and stark,
Do they know where I've parked my car in the dark?
The moon just chuckles, like a wise old sage,
"Embrace the absurdity; it's all the rage!"

So here's my map, it's a scribble of fun,
A treasure hunt journey under the sun.
With laughter as my guide and cheer in my stride,
Let's navigate life on this absurd ride!

Whispers from Within

There's a voice inside, quite chatty and sly,
It tells me to dance, and I can't deny.
But then it shouts, "Don't eat that cake!"
I nibble it anyway, for goodness' sake.

With giggles and chuckles, my thoughts parade,
"Why take the stairs when you can upgrade?"
This inner monologue, a playful jest,
Keeps me entertained, oh, what a quest!

Sometimes I ponder, what wisdom to seek,
While chasing my tail, feeling quite chic.
That whisper suggests a roundabout dance,
Spinning in circles, isn't life just a chance?

So here we are, with whispers and cheer,
Laughing at nonsense, that's crystal clear.
Embrace the whispers, and let 'em be wild,
For life feels like play, when you're a curious child.

Fragments of a Distant Dawn

Morning breaks with a clatter and clang,
I rise from my bed, still tangled in slang.
The sun yells "Hello!" with a warm, silly grin,
While I search for my glasses, where have they been?

The day stretches out like a cat in the sun,
Filled with odd puzzles and a dash of fun.
I juggle my coffee, a balancing feat,
Wishing life's mysteries were sweet and of wheat.

Each moment presents a mismatched sock,
As time proves to be a slippery clock.
Fragments of thoughts dance on the breeze,
Tickling my mind with playful tease.

So here's to the dawn, all quirky and bright,
Chasing fragments of laughter throughout the night.
With a chuckle, a wink, and a jolly old cheer,
Let's toast to life's riddles, both far and near!

www.ingramcontent.com/pod-product-compliance
Lightning Source LLC
Chambersburg PA
CBHW071852160426
43209CB00003B/524